THIS SUPER DOOM I AVER

Russell Jaffe

Poets Democracy
Atlanta Miami
Chicago Milwaukee

Published in the United States by Poets Democracy.
PoetsDemocracy@gmail.com
Library of Congress Control Number: 2012918877
ISBN: 978-1-937202-06-4

Acknowledgements

Thanks to the editors of American Letters & Commentary, Verse Wisconsin, NOÖ, The Cossack Review, Russ Woods and Meghan Lamb of Red Lightbulbs, Sandra Allen of Wag's Revue, and Erica Mena-Landry of Anomalous Press for publishing poems from this collection, and to CAConrad, a truly amazing human being and superhero who collaborated on "The whole Universe is either one thing or one other thing" on his video journal Jupiter 88.

Also, 1000 XOXOs to the following people who have supported and inspired me: Mom, Dad, Grandma Bev, and B Jaff; John Engelbrecht, Eric Asboe, Lesley Wheeler, and Karl McComas-Reichl; Don Arenz, Blueberry Morningsnow, Tembi Bergin-Battan, David Hulm, Tonja Robins, Al Rowe, Lauri Hughes, and Willie Barbour at Kirkwood Community College; Lucy Lazer, Tyler Luetkehans, Quincy Anna Benton, Nick Demske, Becky Dewing, Steve Pernetti @ Fair Grounds, Rosie Peele, Russell Streur, Laura Hampton, Bruce Jay, and my Write. Poetry. Right. Now! poetry students and friends R.C. Davis, Justine Retz, Chris Eck, Eric Roalson, and Lisa Roberts.

Table of Contents

Participation belly button

Attention. Poke. ____________________________. Bad signal. Redo.
(attention getting noise)

Here's where we fit once. And when we play we'll always remember we did. Remember how hot it was. That summer.

Stuffed animals _______________ faced each other prone on the
(adverb)

floor. And you said that was just OK. Birthday presents? No. The universe gives us one present: flesh, to remind us.

Black hole belly button. __________________________ ice cream
(your favorite nebula)

swirls. You're poking me, I said. No, you said. Present thyself if you're so born. Here's my belly button. That's how you know I'm real and not a clone or anything. This is the Savage Land or Magneto's space base. Or the outer space parts of The Infinity War; those comics have some X-Men in them, I said.

I've never watched X-Men, you said, and then I was watching X-Men cartoons inside. I'm being a boy. And my Ultimate Warrior plush and I were warriors in war. That _________________ could
(noun, green)

only smell like chlorophyll, and everyone laughed. Thanks,

nature, for memories and green so we can separate ourselves from outer space. I'm being a boy again, rushing through spaces of stone suburb backyard shed meteor ________________ poop
(large pet)

walking paths. I count myself as spider webby as crystalline hornet's nests. Technicolor void ice cream hot day childhood

________________________. Eventually you come back to that
(something that spirals)

walking shape. Like how taking a summer road trip together, my

_________________, was like driving at night through the
(pet name)

____________________ roads versus looking at the light green hash
(noun, boundary)

mark section of a map. Dad has to work outside, so come in. I was little, and I did. And my parents, like yards, chores, and dinner around mosquitoes that hung in the air like Styrofoam ball mobiles of find-it-yourself galaxies, were around. The war is waiting. And you were back to your _________________ in your
(craft project)

childhood basement near a wooded area upstate. And as you slept in your mother screamed at your father.

How she screamed. And you clutched a ____________________. But
(stuffed animal)

here's what was unsettling about that story of that summer you told this summer: It's the kind of non-human origin story of

a(n) ____________________. By being _____________, it makes me.
(object of worship) (you)

A Bedazzler is still a gun. Action figures faced off. That weapon-scented artillery pounding of the head, those fingernails against the glass eyes of plush friends. Faster ______________.
(artillery)

Pounding on the wall. Pounding wake up on the door. Cannons blasting again and again. The human belly button. Touch the hole left alack, feel kaboom. And it was unsettling because you learned to roll your eyes. Touch touch. And you were never afraid. You and your mother. And room and the hallway. And that was a decade ago. Actually, you decide: pit them. That was X ago. That was you-choose-now: This stuffed toy is a funny friend. Thus we're allies. The _______________. The summer infinity conflict.
(warzone)

The ____________ war. The X war. The X X.
(gender)

Apocalypse fistpump

Go ____________ yourself. For you are a—wait for it—
(auger)

construction. You have the bodily countenance of a pile of construction equipment in the moonlight. What a(n)

__________________ thing to say. By __________ we are more
(adjective) (time)

vexed. By day we are boards, fences, bloodlettings.

I do street art of mystical ohms and you wouldn't get me.

Paint this _______ and call it the new flesh.
(color)

This is the unification no-man's zone between language and the body, though the skull is always less so. In my guts I kill the debris. It's my only filter. I'm super pumped for the apocalypse. I'm not a fate type. My new flesh is cultural implications of poetry sewn together with pipecleaners and fake flowers. Someone died here, isn't that ________________? Check it out: an idol.
(adjective)

Fistpumps to our collapse for real. These are my conditions of worship:

1.)____

(condition)

2.) ____

(condition)

3.) ____

(condition)

Dear sweet voids

I am ready. You: Ok, so write a book about it. Me: Ok, I will.

It will have poems.

Eventually there'll be

____.
(futuristic form of communication)

For now, I send ________________ emails into the void.
(number, huge)

Dear voices, I hope you enjoy the following poems:

____.
(poems)

Dear voids, you are where my friends were. You wouldn't believe what we have in the future past. Epitaphs of all our friends. I am here. If my book fails, __________. If it is the greatest, mark my
(fate)

epitaph with ____________________________________.
(the greatest compliment)

I have a crashed airplane ego and freewheelin' doom on the mind—recognize. I have nothing but the courage to _________ it
(verb)

all and write poems to this wreckage.

The greatest contribution of my generation is the trope, duh. And

what's every boy's dream?

To see the wreckage of your prophets laid before you, obvs.

I await your

reply.

Participation guts /pet moth Glidey, may you bludgeon the dream of the poem always

My pet moth, amen. I had one. Glidey. Please write what you'd like to say to him, my teacher said when he died the week he was born. The last lines I wrote about him then in first grade were "I will love you forever." Polyphemous moth, a big one with milky bulbs like the eyes of the ready to die dead. Grandpa died. Your turn: I ask you under a bright lamp outside a strip mall bar about your better nights. You tell me your dreams are a rotoscope of clichés. To repeat is to kill, always, always, amen. There are things in the parking lot of the Pizza Ranch I threw bottles at, but now my sobriety is the double fisted kind, the flightless afraid but beady-eyed kind. We watched them. Together we are warm beds we call graves. The sun invited the clouds over to tell bunk bed stories. Bla bla bla. Yakkity yak yak yak. Flutter, flutter, there, there. Please write what you said here:

____

____

____

____

____

____.
(eulogy)

The funeral march is so awesome. I can lower my head and sway with it and no one can say otherwise. I don't know how many times I thought it at grandpa's funeral, how many times back when I reminded my brother about when the clouds were breaking, when the Are You Afraid of the Dark episode with the dream machine came on that scared him. Fear. Some. I count myself among those who turn away from beaches in favor of sandbox-side swimming pools. You said I was a poet. But I am forever too bludgeony. What would you like to be? And would you believe the romance of an abandoned walkie talkie in the sand? And I was sleepy. And will you dance to the anthem of my manifesto? Write an apology for every oceanside star or useless streetlight, aggressively catch a ________________, tie it to
(night bird)

it. This is the way I held you. Curled over we played a kind of family van smooth jazz leaving the funeral. Then,

_______________________ was a swansong, but pwish pwish was the
(fighting sound effect)

sound of Ninja Turtle figures punching with tremendous loft. Now

I warn you with a _______________ warble at anonymous pizza
(day bird)

restaurants. Grandpa called me generational so I played on his

computer and ate most of the food in his house, RIP, amen, amen.

Now I have his sweaters. Never liked birds.

If you catch me writing about birds, please kill me. X my eyes.

At night when the _____________________ took to the streets we cut
(people or animals)

the heads off the birds and sent their guts forevermore down the

streams of the gutters, amen.

May we invade the dreams of our loved ones always.

You will see such pretty things

"You will see such pretty things"-Wyoming Incident (TV station hijacking)

I like signals. I like ________________.
(you)

You will see such pretty things.

I like the idea of DOOM more than the actual video game, which is terribly repetitive. I wrote in the booklet under the notes section "every pixel a ______________________." Butterflies are certain
(something precious)

kinds of pretty things. There are others. You fell asleep on your stuffed pony. Daffodils in empty vodka bottles. Wet grating above basement storm windows. Indoor kid smells. Playstation. A station where you can play? Pretty. Basement walls. I remember how pretty you looked. Don't worry, I remember. I'll have a(n) ______________________ implanted into my
(electronic/reminder)

______________________ to remind me.
(unselfish body part)

Who needs friends when you've got a ______________ of bitter regret?
(vessel)

"None of you understand. I'm not locked up in here with you. ***You're*** *locked up in here with* ***me****.".- Rorschach, WATCHMEN*

I owe __________________________ for falling in love with you. This
(social networking site)

is the age of droning. Spoiler alert: this drone is anthemic. I've been wasting my time on airplanes when there are hovercrafts, know what I mean? I use the word realm.

Don't trust your ____________________ or ____________________;
(god) (emperor)

trust tin cans and strings, walkie talkies, anti-frequency "hello? hellos!?" Rec/Mem/Play portraits. I was born to yell and scream.

______________________, won't you let me?
(pet name)

This is my zone and these are my letters from the inside. S.W.A.K.

Hello?

Responding to things fulfills a __________________________.
(primal urge)

Respond. Respond. Reply.

____.
(reply)

I shall apologize now for some of the doom

The future is ______________. This generation's good at all things
(adverb)

wreckage. It's the being ________________________ that's hard.
(positive attribute)

I'm improving. NOT. Or am I? I want brimstone now. I shall

consult the internet, and it shall say, "here is one unexpected way

to burn _______________ fat." Every hole I leave is part of my
(body part)

great crash and burn. Every poem I've ever written has been this

kind of apology:

for saying at a reading in front of ______________________ people that
(number, under 10)

my family "didn't get poetry, so I didn't really share it with them;"

to my insurance company for my frequent and uncomfortable

urination, and why don't I just man up and pay the

$_____________________ bill and enough with the socialism?; to the
(number, over 600)

true Marxists and Jungians and other fans of museum culture,

whose collective consciousness I use a parachute as I jettison this

engulfed cockpit so that I may live some; to epididymitis itself, whose bacteria is trapped mysteriously in me and whose effects may last up to ____________ years. My phone is filled with pictures
(number)

of ______________. I fly. Roads are the most dangerous things in
(ruins)

the whole _____________ing world. I want flaming carnage now.
(swear)

But when you're ready. I'm sorry. NOT. Or am I?

Carnage fetish

We share our body parts, duh. I hate the gendering happening in the phrase, "I love the destroyed wreckage of mankind."

We're such babies to compare the universe to our bodies. I wish it was night over the ocean. So I could see the ____________________
(celestial body)

reflected in the Pacific Garbage Patch. I wish the sun wasn't so

________ing violent. Beat my ___________. Trash piles remind me
(swear) (body part)

I'm alive, part of something. Oh yeah. Here's what the legions of our piled bodies have manifested: Empty bottles. Blood stains. Unrecycled recyclable paper. Diapers. Post-rocket launcher video game fire. You're left shuffling mangled. When I did dishes, the hot water made the cheese become an angel. I identify more with the sleeker, miniature _______________________ than the traditional
(noun, form of doom)

________________. Oh! I recognize humanity in the streamlining.
(torture device)

Got so worked up explaining this that I had to go home and

______________________.
(something)

I'll keep this to myself.

Giant caterpillar sleepover party

Goodbye, dark green dark. Party time. You looked like a caterpillar in your sleeping bag, so we hit you with pillows until you claimed the zipper hit you in the tooth and that's why you cried. Like a moth in the dark you threatened to walk home and take in your surroundings as you did. Cool off, you cocoon gnasher you. There's only one road in or out, buddy. We are so brave to hop loops around you laughing. We put on monster masks and chased you into the streets. When you couldn't hop in your bag you rolled, legs kicking for something to hold struggling on to. You bite, you grow, we chanted. We dragged you back to the basement and stayed up all night yelling our favorite WWF wrestler anthems and flying between dusty basement mattresses, heads cracking the track lights. We caved in the dry wall. We ate everything that looked like a leaf: Bubble Tape, Fruit Roll-Ups, fang after fang of gas station jerky. Why, why did you have to put on porn? We were _____ and when my dad would pick
(age)

me up the next day, he told me about the video tape he found in the drawer next to my bed. Do I have any questions? Yes: may I stay wrapped up forever with my mouth protruding so that Capri Sun and torn shreds of better snacktime floor remains may be sacrificed to it? May I have newer, weirder landscapes now? You finally fell asleep. Everyone did. You aren't like other boys, you were worried, I said to myself. Swishing behind my teeth it was a safe and quiet thing to say. You're too big and like a cylinder. Everyone was asleep then and the TV was a lone tooth poking out of the bottom jaw of a skull no one invited. I am that sometimes. Who will be my girlfriend? Stars beyond the basement grates? The unmoved bikes in the bushes we abandoned temporarily? Girls rolling me between their arms and legs? Girls I roll myself around pressing? Girls pressing girls around me and there'll always be saxophone and the drone of the almost-sun behind the pricier edges of the suburban woods for rich people only? I wandered to the bathroom in the red dark of the off-over-there Chicago sky vs. the tinted house in the woods windows. It may as well be the end of the world you're rolling off, you strange boy, I said to me. I'm glad you didn't hear me. 4 am. 5

am. I'm finally brave. I don't care, bring them both on. Bring on what comes next. Come on! Jerking off over the sink in the wall molding darkness: You may omit these lines if you wish. You may fill the walls with ____________. You may cut these lines but you'll
(filling)

have your own manifesto someday. Look in the mirror. Girls? Nothing but lumps against dark lumps. Chocolate ice cream scoops in Coke. Pines tipped over in the embarrassingly sequestered expensive nighttime. Rumbling nostrils of the suburban tomb our parents birthed us in locked. Lock the door. Look in the mirror. There's a WWF ring covered in blood stains. There's a silver rocket care and a lone road. There's a desert. And everything's so weird and tangled up, and it's always gonna be. Look down into the sink. It's a spike mouthed pit monster. The best monsters have no eyes. I'm back.

Monster ballad

The ________________. Lie: All we have is love. ZZZ. The truth is
(fugue)

that all we have are cans of food and that there are plants and animals. You are free or whatever. I choose to cash in on this by driving. Highway trees remind the sun of bedbugs.

Epitaph one: doom variations. Guitar solo cornstalk hair. So expect locusts on your genomes. You are the worst human traffic cone. We've created a monster. We live on its back. It sleeps so hard things grow on it. Good example. Well well well, if it

isn't ____________________________. Monsters never die hard. Drive
(your favorite monster)

a lone note sun. Nature, you made an awful mistake and I'll never forgive you. Plants subsist in a symbiotic relationship wherein humans cultivate and preserve them and in turn

they teach our doomed brains galactic phenomena

for beginners. Satanic hex.

Hexing slashes to your chainsaw piety.

BUUURRRPPP. Oh, I

______________________.
(apologize)

For being a ________________ of a man. The best monsters have
(beast)

no ________________.
(sense organ)

________________________. I am driving right now. I spend days on
(sinister laugh)

earth. I shall join

you. Mua-ha-ha.

Ha ha ha.

Ha.

Happy birthday: ______________________________ (memory in which you carry yourself)

Be a ______________ of ____,
(vessel) (critical documentation/documents)

but today you're air. I am not here in the fuzzed VHS-ness of

______________________th baby teeth family camera lens birthday
(small age)

parties in ______________________________, so deal with it.
(neighborhood park)

I am not here in the junction of

____ mist
(suburban streets/grass dew/traffic cone)

where ________ is what _____________________ baby teeth in wet
(fear) (lowercase emotion)

park benches do to ______________________________. Therefore,
(environmental phenomena)

upon careful reflection, deal with it.

I compare ______________ to the kind of
(something)

____________________________________ you feel
(lowercase dissonance variation)

when you realize a

____
(terrible noise like when you realize for the first time that helium balloons pop/the kind of elation when helium balloons do that thing to your voice/both of them together)

happens on your better nights entrusted to analog recordings and

basement boxes like the bag of ____________________________ you were.
(selfish organ, plural)

So happy birthday. But for want of the _________________________
(mortal lack)

the _____________ is already dying.
(sky or body)

I shall be free

With artillery. My sad and battle damaged epididymis. My blown out lung breathing exercises. Not now though; then: then we'd cleaned out the garage. Then we'd spent that day learning about the Constitution and all the rules. No punching or slapping.

Arms. My cobweb hanging ____________________. ____________ water
(Super Soaker) (article)

fight. Dad was the general and my brother and I soldiers. Soldier, have one on me. ____________________________.
(beer/wine/spirit)

The general must be overthrown, I told the little solider.

Lie down on the grass. Look, you are gushing blood. That's water, the little solider, whose eyes were, said. No, it's blood.

These are wadded handfuls of your guts, not your wet balled up shirt. The revolution will be ____________________. Weapons go
(wet adjective)

from war to the museum. Rockets are empty missiles. Liquid

____________________ everything at its own pace.
(destroy, plural)

Drink yourself caustic loser of the war. It's super sad to say

“one day you’ll know that ______________ store parking lot.” I
(wine/spirit)

___________ the Constitution sick with my stains,
(verb)

my exhumations like garage toys. But back then I said, little solider, you are back to life. You have the right to bear water. Water cannon. Water grenades. The forlorn neighbor dad goes “I can never do this with my kids.” And for another hour or so it will always be like this. Wonder what he’s drinking.

____. We have the
(joke about too much or not enough of it)

will to never will. Bazooka time. Liquid vs. liquid, liquid passing spots of liquid in the air, the final _____________. This ultimate
(judgment)

war. Too much. _____________ cool. So I don’t talk about
(cannon)

epididimytis or asthma with my dad or brother. The only thing worse than being splattered with blood is never being. My

___________ shall be let loose thus.
(spirit)

Liberation: an elegy

When I ______________________________ elegy, the
(searched-for, in popular search engine verb)

first thing that came up was ____________________. And yet
(first thing that came up)

I shall somehow be the first.

I'll be the first I know with this condition; I'll be the first man on

Jupiter if it crushes me. I'll cut each moon loose. I'll hang

intrepidly the body of myself affixed to the stars' sneezed-on

diorama. I'll glue on the black construction paper and forget.

What will become of me and my testicles if the epididymitis

doesn't go away? My friend says they'll

________________________ them off. Fire the rest of me
(remove, extremely inappropriate)

into space. Set me free from this jet stream of constantly going to

the bathroom. I apologize for when I asked if I was quotable.

When I said quotable I heaven-sent was the porcelain expellant of

the gods. Until the ______________ or accidental
(antibiotic)

Ibuprofen overdose wore off. And not remembering is what keeps the swelling down. Celestial bodies behold: I am liberated from

______________________________.

(how you feel right now)

I shall play unapologetically

I could just be going crazy. ________________________________. It
(crazy person noises)

could also just be the planets. They paint the dome of the earth like clouds so you won't go crazy. They hang up

__________________________ and blinking lights so you don't feel
(noun, arcade décor)

bad to be among your kind. And you can always win tickets. You can't take your tickets to the afterlife. They encourage you to paint portraits so you won't feel like just a little nothing adrift in the ultimate anti-playzone: the universe, AKA your day. You push through the mesh enclosure until you're face to face with the portrait and then you say: "Hello. This is a condition." Your parent supervises from behind the crossword. When I asked to write a poem about you, I felt ___________________________________.
(feeling you get in a ball pit)

When you said ok it was all ____________ rocket. But the way you
(color)

said it was ____.
(childhood Nintendo game long lost to the annals of time)

Sigh. Another toy chest memory excursion. Another sweet

nothing on the back of straight-to-DVD case. Another dead world. Another portrait of something destroyed. Another

____________________ ____________________. What is the universe
(adjective) (noun)

now to us but a playzone that can't pay the space rental fee? What is this sweet work with if thou kiss me not? As I collapse into colored balls I shall destroy. Whoa! __________________
(exclamation)

Here we go! This town will burn upon atmospheric reentry. I shall be the core of this town and rip it. Onto a DVD. Get your best underwear and dance. These are love poems to the world of direct-to-DVD. You were born to this condition. That's the best lie from your third eye. It's nurture, all nurture. We learned the calligraphy of the ball pit. ____________________. This condition
(exclamation)

is for the direct-to-DVD market in you. It was the market that made me destroy. The destroy made me ____________________.
(emotion)

"What is all this sweet work worth If thou kiss not me?"

for Kevin Olish
"You got the chainsaw." –DOOM (for Playstation)

This is a loop, so love me like one. I love video game areal maps,

you, and blood pixels. Sweet antiquity of once-was-brutal-then,

oh. Kiss me not. Kiss me. Not. Kiss not, me. I confess, outer space

is a human emotion. I am all my lost levels. I am equally old poem

and garden. This is nothing less than the Playstation of the

_________________________ soul. My parents wouldn't let me play
(something that dies)

DOOM or Mortal Kombat, but I can as much as I want now. This

artifice is a content-devoid reward. I only dance in outer space.

You think I'm listening but I'm killing opponents again.

This is a recording. My voice is often a one-way conduit of

manifesto-isms, broken toy memory blues, baby-I'm-sorry's. Little

beautiful, if you are fake then all of this is fake. The gimmick is the

artifice. And what was that word you used for the totality? Oh yes, it

was

____.

(what was the word you used for the totality)

Elegy

I am trying to figure out my role in ______________________________.
(historical preservation, study)

Sometimes I think feelings only exist because

________________________________ wanted to give us a heads up
(nature/universe/personal god)

on what plants we can and can't eat. I worship homemade gods.

Prepare yourself for decontextual reframing. Go. Ahead.

Obvious suggestion to embrace

____

(noun, form of doom)

Begin with satan stars. First, you draw them in the follow-along

__________ of your ______________ of your
(peripherals) (religious document)

________________, the one you get during the service.
(place of religious worship)

Your friends' parents let them play __________
(handheld game)

when things get super boring. It's not that you are filled with

____________, but that you just don't like the way.
(noun, form of doom)

And no girls grab ________________ you and play
(teenage adjective)

with your ________________ or tell you your
(body part [innocent])

____
(article of clothing grandma got you but you hate to wear because
it's uncomfortable and makes you stand like the road fawns just
over the highway and then into panic pouring into the wooded suburbs)

makes you look funny or smile with hair and eyes.

Satan stars to them all. Satan stars go in the

____________________________pages of
(publishing ephemera)

____
(comic strip compendiums, most likely involving witty cats)

you check out from the ___________________________ library. Then in
(junior high grade)

your locker, on your ankles, wrists.

Satan star and you-will-be-________________________________. Spend
(noun of damnation)

the day in _____________ shirts, solid black ones, even if you've never
(band)

heard them. Pimples. You're overeating because you just want to

kiss someone so bad. Then spend the night with a bottle of

____
(inexpensive gas station beverage, the more colorful the label the

_________ in front of ____.
better) (Social networking site/literary blog)

Too late. Your coffin will be a cocoon of paper mache articles

about the new generation of

____ one day. Your epitaph
(smug faced, arm crossed entrepreneurs)

is an art class erasure of________________________________
(mid-late 90s video game system)

game box descriptions. Will poetry help? Your life will be a decay-

friendly auto-pictography of unmade

________________________________ shirts. For now,
(print-on-demand website)

________________________________ fits loose and baggy,
(teenage colloquialism)

loves like you do, longs, dies, is—just wants to feel what is is.

Today

Our breakfast condition. Maritime clouds suggest bombs of rain.

Clouds, a polemic of white balloons. Share with me your dream. I

extend my gaze. You rebuke.

Wilt. __________________________. Bla bla bla. Today I dreamt we
(something natural)

dreamt something.

____.
(please share your dream)

Anti-matter-of-fact

Hopefully the very idea of me should explode you. At my funeral, I'd like a "best in the world" chant.

If not for the finality, for the fact that I want the cadence of an outdoor pro wrestling show. Listen to me, ________________.
(top deity)

I am white, I have a beard, some of my shirts are flannel. I hate that about myself. I will attend to this matter of what I am. If

I lose __________ lbs, I'll be ______ more __________. I should be a
(number) (%) (noun)

giant gay Japanese woman pro wrestler. Then I would have odds to overcome and a more explainable reason to cry about feeling like the odds exist and I have had to overcome them.

PS: Since I am explaining, I am here. I am here. I am ____________.
(here)

Etc.

I miss the wild ______________________________ public access TV
(local pro wrestling company)

ego trip. I thus became anti- __________________. I am the rainy
(programming)

dishes on suburban roofs, so.

The bulbous night rejected me. Not the other way around. Thanks for leaving a little nature for me to be roadside lonely in. That is to say: they shouldn't call it night—too angular. Maybe something rounder, like stubble. They cut all the trees down on this bald point of an end of the world. Dead highway river parallel drips from your chin, a fatal blow. Night loop-de-loops my trackless walks and I get lost in there like

a ______________ hole. I patch the rolling casket of my face with
(color)

notepad pages and ______________________, I've been brawling. This
(someone, anyone)

is a meditative there-there, ________________________________ to
(compliment)

the comic-book-and-yearbook-diary-page interdimensional gateway. Never asked. I wish more people liked me and this right here is dedicated to the highway divider between what I am and what I'll never be. Big bang blow ups are always such an emotional end of me. I was upset because I thought everyone had accidentally learned to worship gods of coincidence.

I was so worried about the suddenly of it all.

Now, I'm anti-alcohol, anti-drugs, anti-hate,

anti-______________________, anti-
(positive attribute)

____________________, anti-name-something-and-I'll-be-anti-it.
(matter)

Then

Wild ________, we laughed into you like Wrestlemania and the
(year)

faces and the hair that framed faces that held big glasses and the

colorful shirts. ________________________. Like a WWF ring playset
(crowd noises)

covered in superheroes flying, attacking, prolonged,

________________. I'll come over after the next match and I'll never
(preparedness)

stop. We're forever around. Don't kick me out of your

__________________________________.
(most secret zone w/ posters)

I don't want to drape myself in your father's nightshade of sports

equipment. I don't want to hide in your mother's medicinal tile

and plant ______________________. Just the one.
(fortress)

But I always hated black and white tile and I always felt nauseas

in waxen spotlights. I always

____.
(you and the way you feel)

They saw me leave. And they asked me about school and if I'd lost

weight and if I knew even though Hulk Hogan had won the belt again. I decline in every way. I want to be your VCR. I want to be your drop top lo-fi. I want to be your MEM like a man. I want to kiss you like Rowdy Roddy Piper. Or not. Or.

We're not

not special.

I want real ice cream. In a dream cone.

I am trying to figure out my role in historical preservation. I asked once but it keeps walking by busy and I felt shy to ask again. So on this misty galaxy nebula milky fog in go-to-school, USA, I wait for the bus. Stories. ________________________. Among the
(baby star just born)

cover of fussy planets and their tote-along moons I am privy to this wait-for-the-bus condition. I do the backpack and raincoat twirl alone until I become ________________________.
(ice cream and topping)

I have some time to think about the ________________________.
(ice cream flavor)

Lick one. A reason to continue. All that is human is a cone. But a dream cone. I hope you'll say all that is sweet. Lick two. Be sweet. I'll dip life's cone in sprinkles and hope the knowledge sticks. I hope the knowledge doesn't make a gloppy white puddle, also. The sliver of my jacketed face lit by unknown suns is embarrassed by light poles. I was zipped too tightly into this condition. Pejorative discourse upside down on the pavement of the ______________________________, astral-project
(suburban streets intersection)

me from here. Or I'll go to sleep and be a baby star exploding born

every day. Or ______________trying.
(fate)

All hail the new flesh

I said the first person shooter was the new flower. The new

_______________. The new _______________.
(void) (currency)

The avant-rocket-launcher/squirt gun. The controller cable is the new thrift-store autoerotic suggestion. Use the direction pad/joystick to twirl your character. Look up. Ha.

You're dancing.

I shall manufacture a litany, and there shall also be a little doom

A prayer: May I not be crazy for crazy's sakes. I will not be cuckoo

for ____________. For heaven's sakes stop whining about
(the noises)

everything. You are so needed. Like snow. Like the copy of

Writer's Market I saw on a background shelf in a porno movie.

Or like brimstone. The key to being human is documentation.

This drive is worth it. This job is worth ___________. The cars
(it)

honk like geese over oil fields. Helicopters.

Once I recovered from the symptomatic loss of everything, I was

free to __________.
(?)

Drive through American I-beam wasteland distances,

________________ outskirts, USA, PO Box ____________________.
(American city) (bad luck number)

Winter may render the doomed pornographic.

When snow spray paints the insides of concrete it's derivative.

I make snow devils. Nothing's sadder. You don't have the muster

to call yourself displaced. Aver. We have the best ruins in the whole universe. If you're sad and lonely use your

____________________ to render the ____________________ boyesque
(weapon) (settlement)

a simple carnage. There's no bomb that can't be resold on ebay. I got rid of everything I could and smiled with the googly eyes of the damned. A manifesto, like a giant caterpillar, became a litany, like a giant moth trapped in huge glass bowl. Inconvenient sky. Your prayers are so vulgar and your suffering is all for

____________________. Clutch your clumsy portraiture of live
(nothing, noun)

burials. Speak to the judgmental stars.

I'll cull cereal, teenage sick days, American Gladiators, wood panel wallpaper. And broken-hinged TV dinner trays, bunk beds for one. TV static is my home turf. This winter's collectable cadaver is that of my kindest ____________________. Trudge lightly.
(barren wasteland)

Ain't no thing but a Satanic hex. Choose your barren hellscape. As if in polar environmental extremes carry like an idol your portraiture away. Clutch it tightly, for we are almost at

___________________________. At least you are.
(promised land)

But I am the blatantly symbolic effigy in this picture.

Outer space and other thrift stores

A dislodging. Remove the ink cartridges and see what your

stained hands say back. The tall poles and signal lines like old

rails. The ________________________ and the other side
(favorite tree in fall)

of black holes. The static I dreamed was superior to nature.

Space TV shows may make you consider the TV oracular on

inkspot nights like these, but not for the lack of thrift store

printer. Explode the shopping day with a stalled night as uselessly

defamiliarizing as ____
(how you feel when you click "who is this person" cheap website advertisements and answer them incorrectly on purpose)

Thrift store after thrift store.

I buy stuffed animals for the party. Thrift store after thrift store.

The ____ of it all.
(the way you feel about the furthest-out strip malls)

Will one collide into ________________? I float like globs of kind
(favorite planet)

liquid in the vacuum. That is nice. My manifesto smeared to my

mortal ________________hands, the earth is a plush's eye.
(a chaining)

Print-your-own manifesto big as _________________________.
(galactic phenomena)

And this is also the night of that forest party with the paintings

nailed to the trees. ____.
(line that connects all this to outer space)

There were spinning leaves and a mud fire pit I threw dirty

stuffed animals into. Evacuate, memory. Jet streams of halo

light where the hole once was. __________________________________.
(something about infinity)

Destroy because.

Space is ____. You still
(space noun/space verb/space adjective)

have to know when to drift.

When to stand and when to begin to walk. Or

you don't.

re: Voices

_______________’s insanity is, according to Wikipedia, a matter of
(dictator)

contention among __________________ historians. When I tell
(ancient culture)

people I’m not crazy, I think immediately that that sounds crazy.

When I tell them *that* sounds crazy, I wait a beat and say,

“but I’m actually not. I know crazy. ___________________________.”
(crazy person noises)

This super doom I aver

Doom on you.

Doom is topical and I want to be topical. Rub me all over you.

_________________. I was lazy. I was scared of__________________________.
(emoticon) (galactic phenomenon)

That's how I knew love. I was all tired out from playing board games with companion video cassettes. It was a long, magnetic tape weekend with sticky _______________ hands from when you
(fruit juice)

bite that fruit hard enough. You are all gluey then in your doom and have to go outside to shake it off. I took a little journal and wrote about the telephone wires and the lawn furniture. Then I wrote about the face of the water. ________________ is the best
(water word)

word. Yes. Naptime alert. But still there was the matter of the

________________ face in the water. Back awake and gluey
(adjective)

I called up some friends and said we'll get all crazy around the fire tonight. I brought a bag of ___________________________ to burn.
(significant documents)

The fridge leaked blood and there was a banjo playing. A phone was ringing and we couldn't believe it was a land line. That's an

umbilical cord under plastic wrap in the fridge. That's how we

saved the cord blood. Dear friends, we are reminded.

Today we are born today again, we are. Aren't we? Yes,

I just said so. I documented. If I find this taxonomy to be pollution,

I'll stop, I swear, under heavy sanctioning. We put hexes on

organic trash (like fruit rinds and seeds). We burned arts

and literature because we are right ____________ing now. Despite
(swear)

out best efforts. Or

worst. The fire cooked the wood into outer space. I want to know

what it felt like to be the first person on fire. Did they go after

water? There's nothing funny about that. Organic. Plunging my

hands in, I pulled out the organ. Ick. Bedtime alert. Tomorrow.

Today. No more jokes. Stand and _______________ with me. ZZZ.
(verb)

Dear friends, I'm sorry I deserted you. Back out of bed I play the

cassette without the board game. I sat down with my working

manifesto with ____
(title from a poem you've written)

as the working title. I found the page with the writing about the

face of the water and wrote

this doom

a super doom.

Ya Doomsayer, ya lousy Doomsayer

"Don't be scared, homie!"-Nick Diaz

I wish that during a ____________________, the commentator'd say
(sporting event)

"Well, we have no rhyme or reason to our lives, none at all, everything is conjecture and for all our mortal foibles with documentation, we've made no ripples cosmically whatsoever." But in a really sportscastery voice. Is my dandruff stars or bug eggs? ___________________________. I see bugs everywhere,
(Well? Which?)

under my skin, laying eggs in dents in the sky, and suddenly I'm the crazy one? Naw, ________________. It ain't like that.
(animal)

If the entire universe works on a series of rotation-based spirals and takes nature down in a grinding _____________________
(submission hold)

demanding it do the same, I, affixed and tapping out to circular patterns or something, want to be the 360 degree rotating joystick on a fighting game; you, the big red button that makes you do ___________________________. I'm falling apart and I don't
(something)

care. Only the people who really care a lot dare say they don't care. Still don't care. Dear sun worshipper, your smile could melt me. That should definitely get you going out with me. I wish I were _____________bruised. My face is a coincidence of planets.
(more/less)

If the universe has it figured out, what's with all the punching, then? Maybe it has to do with ________________________________.
(axiom)

But you have the best frown. It's so

inner child. We are paper mache bureaucracies and fight contracts. *That's* crazy. Now fill out this form, negate your polarity, knock your axis off. You have been warned.

Participation brain/Poem beginning with butterflies

In ancient Greek the word for butterfly is "Psyche"...There is also an Irish saying that refers to the symbolic meaning of butterflies. This saying is: "Butterflies are souls of the dead waiting to pass through purgatory"- "What is the symbolic meaning of a butterfly?," Answers.com

Butterflies. But really it's up to you. Choose whenever.

I cannot stress enough that I don't drink anymore because we

drank enough ______________ flavored vodka that night to be
(flavor)

massacre hatchets and one of us got l lost in the bushes between

the house and the neighbor's house where she puked up pink glue

until it was runny. Impending doom is the theme of this party.

So bust out the kiddie pool and plastic tipped mini-cigars. We

spun, we spun. Such ______________ in the night.
(beasts)

I wore a red white, and blue ________________________________.
(head adornment, nostalgic)

Black branches kicking themselves for what could have been.

Butterflies. Are we a hive brain or is mine just super heavy?

Puking into bramble in the hot wind. Ink wires made a misplaced

calligraphy around the yard which was like a cardboard sign.

Black moths moved like the ducks from ______________________
(video game, nostalgic)

on the TV in the dimmer switch living room. Turns out they were butterflies. They always had been. Someone said stallions, but I know we aren't horses, we're ponies because someone else said ponies don't grow. That's the big difference and we laughed about it until someone dropped a quarter onto my teeth. And when we tipped over the table of cards into the bushes we really laughed like wet shoes and old computer garages. Speak for me, truncated necessities. My peeling longitudes of skin; our skulls heavy with brain. I cannot stress enough that I have never been skinny. Coils, tubes, and wires. Water, hair follicles, and flight. We're very

____________ but don't look good on the page. So break out
(adjective)

the waterlogged stationary. Dear____________________________,
(butterflies, to you)

go for it—flooded ___________________________, drink us in.
(time/place, nostalgic)

Participation

I am what ground you left me. I am the ____________________________
(adjective, destroyed)

sugar ______________ dreams of sure, sure, I don't have time today.
(candy)

I don't believe in time, just priorities. This is a condition. I picked it/you picked it. My spirit shape is a falling funnel. My spirit function is a nail. I spike you. That's participation. Me: I'm going to write really short stories. ____________________: Was that one of
(you)

them? Us: High five.

My manifesto

If you write more poems than me, I will drive my tensed hands

like meteors into your guts and then ______________________________.
(outer space catastrophe)

We are such weapons Medieval spike-ball weapons,

____.
(whatever those things are called)

Micro globs of fine pepper spray. The human eye. The listening

ear. You to me are the effervescent thrill of Bubble Bobble: The

Arcade Game. But you are a better listener. I'm noisy. The arcade

screen has ______________________. And us. The little crest
(wobbly light shapes)

of the _____________ universe. I'll pop the bubbles like I'll beat you
(blobbiest)

down, you. You soda bloodstream.

____. If
(something about the universe/galaxies vs. atoms/ions)

you plan to write a bunch of poems you'd best arm thyself.

This is a manifesto in repetition ion by ion: Don't. Never. Never.

Never. My hands are claws that are warhammers to fine china.

I drop. I cut myself open with the pieces. Remove my

____________ bladder. Remove my varnish-tainted
(adjective)

stomach. Out goes the stuffed animal fluff blood.

____
(gross line about eyeballs popping into white liquid and wooly tufts of

____.
thread)

Remove wobbling chunks of congealed blood made that way by

drinking too much seltzer. Bubbles.

______________________________. Brain bubbles.
(the violent sound of being human)

Manifesto: I will outright outwrite. You: take note.

____
(notes)

____
(notes)

____
(notes)

____
(notes)

____
(notes)

____
(notes)

(notes)

(notes)

The whole universe is either one thing or one other thing

Memory, sweet gauntlet. Darkness which is so cockamamie in its

human _______________ness interplay of—wait for it— symbols.
(swear word)

Light which curses the ____________________ blinds. And it's always
(workplace)

one or the other, my doomed humans. And when the universe

blows up small parts of itself it's laughing because we are so

_______________. Knowledge is a just-so explosion.
(adjective)

Sometimes I've only known two things: work and otherwise. And

I am scared. I really did believe life began with C: on the upstairs

computer, which dad called sea shift colon. I identify with

learning games, heavy pixilation, and suburban no-coasts.

I tremble for a future raised by X-Box Live_____________________.
(downloadable content)

I shake for a future that doesn't know the Macaulay Culkin

double-hand-face-slap-AHHHHHH. Beautiful forever beautiful

_______________________________ dear diary.
(name you'd give your diary)

But that's just the me talking. Youth aloof, cross

the______________________.
(coding patterns)

Safety always bludgeons dreams into ____________________________.
(bloody pulp)

Come home thus.

Really looking forward to doom

So we document. Your oft-poetic take on cultural historiographies is super annoying. We'll write ourselves together.

Chapter ___________:
(number)

I'll never live in outer space, but I'm ok with that. Frontier destiny, I miss you. Our new history is avant-doom. I'll wreck your _________________ condition with my
(sun adjective)

toys. If you accuse me of conjecture, I'll show you videos of guys getting punched in the dick. Our shared memory is slouching cassette towers no-no-zones. It's sunset. Been there

______________________________. What we don't say is the shape
(axiom)

of space. BREAKING NEWS: My dad just used "apparently it doesn't come with a

warrantee" as a punch line. _____________________. Sometimes I
(laughter)

think we'd be better off not. It's the 2012 apocalypse with spaceships and floods and gravity. I grab and kiss you desperately. You're a boat now. You're a steel case. A coffin.

You're a life raft. Your guts are magnetic tape. All the rising world

is stained black. You're a mess.

A sudden nebula and our torn organs; the exploding sun, our baby

star, ourselves—

we raise our bright arms to it.

Sadness: the poem: the ride

I was reading about plane crashes today. Is there any more beautiful a eulogy than "He had a passion for small, experimental aircraft?" Is there any afterburner more______________________
(adjective, explosive)

than teenage notebooks with pop star names etched in marginalia? The awful truth is that I found Lindsay Lohan's CD in a ______________ bin. I found my teenage notebooks. You are a
(thrift store)

butterfly. You wear pretty makeup.

"I hope I am as pretty for you as you could dream"—Grandma, in her teenage letters. Grandma, ________________, actually referred
(age, over 85)

to herself today as "old fashioned." "Hey, just writin u back.

____."
(writing)

Bla bla bla. I can be gone. I repeat my hands into

______________________. Today a package came for
(fluttering animal)

______________________. I left it for her. It was more makeup.
(girlfriend name)

She had begun to buy tons of makeup. It covered every room. Towers of makeup boxes topped with open missile silos of lipstick. "I love our armistice," I wrote to her. I left the letter in her pile of CDs and aerial photography books. "All this makeup?" I asked. "Did you read my letter? Will we be forever in love?"

________________________. "Flight," she said. "These are boxes of me.
(sound of loud tears)

These are all could-bes," she said.

I shall remember you like this/Sorry for your doom

So what you did was you grew up cataloguing integral things.

Video tapes that ____________ floors into black mounds. Handfuls
(verb)

of dirt pressed into heaps called

landscaping. Squares of grass unassumingly were laid. Your

father, shaking, paid __________________ workers with a big-
(ethnic minority)

screen hurry-up expression on his face. He told them he'd see

them time and pointed at a patch of branches. The leaves were

a black canopy of marginalia. Hardly anyone ever saw him.

There's nothing like when yard sprinklers hit a passing hearse.

It's a ______________ slow motion amen
(slow noun)

to every point on every star on every flag every summer.

Glass doors closed early and often. Mail order catalogs and

installation discs fell to their knees in the trees. You bury your

____________ out there. Remember that:
(pet)

It would have been funny if there hadn't been so many

__________________ like ship hulls poking up from the sea
(bones)

that's an outer space black hole with worm stars.

___________________ electric cursive art that leave the marks of
(adjective)

their nails as figure 8s in the 80 in 80s. There were mites and

deer ticks that would hold on and dig in. Closets lined with

women's blazers with shoulder pads that smelled like milk. Jerry

Garcia ties, surrender flags over loafers. "Who let the dogs out?"

by Baha Men, *the* dark sonata for parked cars in ______________
(organ)

shaped driveway darkness enclaves. Chicago Bulls fan

parking only, ___________ head, and don't forget your messiah(s).
(swear)

Walk back to my car with me, I'll tell you in hums and pocket

_____________ about cigarettes and girls whose bodies I notice
(noises)

secretly changing. Whose mounds and hills are becoming to me

like Spring. Spring's dirt ____________________________and
(black, or another color)

harder. Tonight it is night bathed, wet-fur shaken stars. Come

with me. I'll tell you about capfuls of ____________________and my
(spirits)

friend's home. They day they put the carpet in it smelled like the front seat of an SUV. We counted our spit liquids among the jetstreams of cinnamon toothpaste, yellow loogies,

_________________________ and little teen beard trimmings like
(very gross thing)

creeks of broken eyebrows in the sink. The marble floors were cold like Spring moss and the way your toes grow into it, never just walking above it. There's always much more than just shoes. Drive home between 2 and 3 am and you won't be hungry. You'll think of slot machine coin sunsets and angular guitar solo sunrises. Also, you'll be alone. You'll lick your lips and taste cigar death, you'll look back and see sirens flashing

________________________ in the forest.
(misdemeanor crime)

Clothes piles grow like ______________________ no one dares ask
(very gross thing)

their stories. They close their windows and tape boxes of video tapes shuts. Drive off to trees that are

__________ mountains and you'll almost forget you did. You'll be
(color)

gone then for even a moment. Hit bumps and your car skips songs endlessly into the night. Crickets angrily rub their legs to a

crescendo. The CD ends but the mixtape is yours. Hold on

to this and look at the rows of pines' wooden teeth shining back

from the sides of the road. We'll stand like logs, we'll be squat

and majestic here, and we'll never go away. We'll always

deteriorate into something new and wonderful, Each Spring

they'll chase us out anew. I'm not arrested, time is. Walk through

my old bedroom, go through my stuff,

you'll see.

A serenely new hell

for Lesley Wheeler

Beloved, the circles of hell look more like a ____________________
(body part, taboo)

than I'll write or read aloud. I'm taking my bad attitude and

impending doom to Twitter and leaving it up for at least enough

minutes for ____spindly demons
(number of Twitter followers of the beast)

to retweet screenshots. I never left poetry, poetry took my face

and ran off into the night with my car keys with the bottle opener

and thumb drive. Joyrode those nighttime one-lane suburbs and

parked in front of one of the big houses with a lot of property and

billboard-sized cutouts of the actual summer

______________________. We died and went to black and white tiled
(summer noun)

floor and high ceilinged ______________________. Statues in
(afterlife)

gardens...ain't that always the way? Demons, turn the lights off

when you park. When your ex-beloved says,

"I just want to figure out who I am besides ___________________'s
(you)

girlfriend," what do you do? Stop being ___________________? No,
(you)

reader, homie, lover, you do not

you say, ________________. Not quite funny enough to laugh, but
(funny word)

funny enough to title a blog after. Ha ha, motherfucker, watch me

doom myself, and yes, these circles do descend into one another,

why? When she says, "I feel like I am ________________'s sidekick,"
(you)

does __________________ respond from within this circle that he
(martial artist)

indeed does not kick, but punches? Macho Man Randy Savage said,

"(she's) going this way, I'm going that way.

OHHHHH YEAAAAAH!"

At Macho Man's age, Macho Man's feet don't leave the ground.

________________ lurches this circle, stalks periphery, designs and
(you)

facilitates new pits, coordinates the literary doom scene, rides a

bike with a basket made of fire now,

gnaws the heads of other available traitors. Speaking as such,

I love

you so ________________________.
(adverb)

New flesh

"All hail the new flesh"-Videodrome (1983)

When I go, please describe me as "disturbing(ly) techno surrealist" (Wikipedia). I never considered friends of family dirt piles but I'm always looking for accidents. Piles of clothes. Piles of dishes. Piles of dishes with crumbs on them between clothes. Piles of cassette tapes and VHS tapes. Piles of 8-tracks. Piles of makeup in a small bag with drawings of ________________on it.
(electronics)

Burned piles of art and literature. Remind me to friends: I was a man who drank ______________. I was a 20-something-
(liquid)

you're-supposed to ___________________________________. I was
(thing 20-somethings do)

educated and alone. I was a man of ________________Facebook
(small press)

comments. Coffin of weather stripping and magnetic tape. Chapter one. Piles of stripped paint and lawn care equipment spit

________-________ fade. To the arcade, remembrance-style today.
(color) (color)

Then we went in our funeral clothes. I have a girlfriend. Stripped naked we spin with the sunlight as tops until the overturned

static goes digital TV blue. A blur, I am so _______________ing
(swear word)

glad. I asked the wires about calligraphy. Day is day, this. Flesh is not my own. Piles of little earth. That's why I moved out of a few cities. That's why I'm not leaving Iowa City. All these medical bills. All the urine I'm producing and my _______________ is not my own.
(organ)

New flesh strange cage. Take my flesh and the effigy of wires is yours to mold into the basement show of everything you haven't done. Your urban decay and subjunctive praising is nothing more than an internet. Your is-it-art-if-the-artist-was-raised-by-the-

_________________________. Youth's threadbare alphabet fails words.
(video game system)

I like to watch TV. Why, what have you heard? We were naked

then. _______________. ___________________ said, when I woke up,
(exclamation) (girlfriend),

"congratulations, you are born!" These TV shows are love poems of genetic memory. For example, no signal. Telephone wires, for example, aren't as impressive when one considers the moon. I offer you the naked hand of my god. You say touchscreen, no. As if

I recalled the cardinal directions like a joystick. The new flesh.

The ____________________________.
(new flesh)

re: Outer space

Now: I shall get a sick tattoo of organs and planets. Then: I was

sent to my room and they'll learn ______________________________.
(threat)

I didn't want pasta anyway and let it go classified cold as

______________________ dead zones. I wept vast like afterburner
(dramatically stark)

jet streams and flairs of a thousand suns. So

I opened my window when I calmed down and I stood on the

roof. It's my time so I'm not listening. Who are you and will you

listen to me? This is my origin story. __________________________
(comic book character)

was strong, so I will be. I hope. Who are you to tell me how to talk

to a teacher? Mom, I cut myself. I'm bleeding.

Here: Fill in tests black as holes and get ____________________
(ADHD pills)

white as teacher hair nebulas and the papers she knocked off my

desk are solar as the wind that blows the playground crater

__________________________.

(galactic phenomenon)

I stretched my can across the known universe.

There's another can at the end.

From the wire I hung the planets and handfuls of lesser lit stars.

I knock them and spin them. "You have the size of the planets wrong," teacher said. "You have the order mixed up," you told me at a party. The ice clinked between beats of M(ercury)y V(enus)ery E(arth, where I built this)ducated M(ars)other J(upiter)ust S(aturn)erved U(ranus)s N(epture)oodles &(just the symbol is better, not an A[nd, could be asteroid belt, rocks hung from a real leather belt in the far-out colder zones]) P(luto)asta. Wrong. Pluto lost its planet status in 2006 and was sent to its room for reconsideration time. They were wrong then. Many versions/exceptions might just step up (for) noodles. Incorrect. Close, but no cigar. False. Just noodles now. They're the wiggly plumes of smoke outside that night, then. A conversation.

We talk elementary school until the strands pull wormhole theory like memories of full recycling bins in the dark. Ha ha, I am still not better. This origin story is sinister.

The sneeze of stars across the dimly lit suburbs of our mortal

galaxy. My little blood stains. Such ______________________.
(annoying qualities)

Stupid universe. Blood-screaming ____________ me is asleep
(animal)

now. Zzz.

Then.

I shall diddle myself

"The smoke of my own breath,
Echoes, ripples, buzz'd whispers, love-root, silk-thread, crotch and vine..."
–Walt Whitman

Earth: I have an announcement to make:

____________________________________.
(announcement)

Nothing's crazier than making choices. This is some kind of

catastrophe. Playtime. Does this vegetarian diet agree with you?

Someone out there owns your ____________.
(DNA)

Just ask all the vegetables. The cultivation of the new has resulted

in animals that produce their own pesticides.

The earth is screaming to stop slamming

a _______________ on its _______________. I have a toy chest full of
(covering) (limbs)

marionette pieces.

I taste like _____________ but will ______________________ you. Play,
(joy) (verb, to injure)

playtime. Mountains are high enough, thank you. Nature: the

ultimate toy chest. Reach in: pull out a _________________. Remove
(toy)

its ________________. Begin now.
(limbs)

Me: Still I am going to write really short stories.

You: Is this one of them? Us: High five.

La, la, la. ______________________. Just diddling myself is all.
(song you sing alone)

__________________. This is the part of you that shouts
(explain yourself)

______________________ from behind the closed door of a busy
(crazy noise)

coffee shop's bathroom. I'm going crazy. ___________________
(crazy person noises)

Your turn.

Russell Jaffe holds an MFA in Poetry from Columbia College Chicago ('08) and is the founder and editor of Strange Cage (strangecage.org), a poetry chapbook press that also curates a reading series. He is the author of the chapbooks *DOOM'D: zones 1 + 2 ('12)* and *so manifestoxoxo* ('11), both published through Strange Cage, (*accompanied by pushpins and balloons)* (The Red Ceilings Press, 11), *LITEROAST* (Counterexample Poetics, '10), and *note/worthy* (Scantily Clad Press, '08). He lives in Iowa City, IA where he teaches a weekly poetry workshop, Write. Poetry. Right. Now!, runs NEW NEW APOCALYPSE: a salon reading series, hosts The Seagull Society monthly storytelling open mic, and volunteers with the Iowa Youth Writing Project. He collects 8-tracks.

www.ingramcontent.com/pod-product-compliance
Ingram Content Group UK Ltd.
Pitfield, Milton Keynes, MK11 3LW, UK
UKHW041925190726
13854UKWH00003B/1441